NO MORE MASK

Living in a World That Profits from Pretending

BY STEPHANIE WILLIAMS, MBA

No More Mask: Living in a World That Profits from Pretending

Published by Booked and Branded Publishing

www.bookedandbrandedpublishing.com

ISBN: 978-1-969369-09-4

Printed in the United States of America

Dedication

This book is for you if you've hidden behind a smile, title, or expectation.

For those who laughed when they wanted to cry, this offers freedom.

For my younger self, the girl striving for perfection, this proves you were always enough.

And to you, the reader, thank you for your courage. By turning these pages, you are proving to yourself that you're ready to live unmasked.

About the Author

Stephanie Williams, MBA, is a strategic business consultant, author, and the founder of Booked and Branded Publishing. Stephanie blends strategy with empowerment, which helps high-achievers, leaders, and creatives shed old narratives and design lives and businesses rooted in authenticity.

Her journey — from corporate boardrooms to entrepreneurship to publishing — revealed both the cost of pretending and the freedom that comes with truth. Now through books, coaching, and speaking, Stephanie equips others with the tools to rewrite their story, build brands that reflect their true selves, and live.

When she isn't writing or consulting, Stephanie is investing in the next generation of leaders and creativity, reminding them that success without authenticity is just another mask.

Tagline: Where hustle meets strategy.

Mission: To help people remove the mask, reclaim their voice, and build futures that feel like home.

Table of Contents

Introduction

We learn to wear masks before we even know we're doing it.

From childhood, people teach us how to earn approval: smile even when we don't feel like it, hide the tears, make ourselves useful, and don't be "too much. "We shift - shape into roles that feel safe — the strong one, the perfect one, the people-pleaser. Each role is a mask.

First, the mask feels protective. It keeps us from judgment, rejection, or punishment. But over time, safety becomes a prison. You wonder: Do people like me — or do they just like the version of me I've been performing?

This book is an invitation to unmask. Not recklessly, but. Not all at once, but piece by piece.

In these chapters, we'll examine the weight of pretending, the mental and emotional cost of carrying old narratives, and the power of boundaries, healing, and redefining success. We'll practice authenticity, not as a trendy buzzword, but as a daily way of being.

Here's what you can expect:

- Clarity on the hidden price of masks.
- Courage to tell the truth, even when your voice shakes.
- Tools for setting boundaries that free your time, energy, and peace.
- Healing for the parts of you that have been silenced.
- Confidence to live — in relationships, work, and life.

The world does not need a better version of your mask. It requires the real you.

And, more importantly, you deserve to be your authentic self.

Let's begin.

Booked & Branded Publishing

CHAPTER 1

The Weight of Pretending

From the moment we wake up, many of us reach for a mask. These are not masks made of fabric or paint. They are invisible ones we have learned to wear, shaped from habits, fear, and expectation. They cover our expressions, our words, and sometimes even our dreams.

Sometimes we smile when we want to cry. Saying "I am fine" is common, yet the truth is the opposite. We nodded in agreement even though our hearts screamed in protest. We stay in jobs that make us miserable, in relationships that wound us, and in roles that shrink us. All because we believe it is safer to conform than to risk rejection.

At first, pretending feels easier. A polite laugh avoids conflict. A cheerful tone keeps the peace. Agreeing with someone earns approval. It can seem like a smart strategy, especially when we are young and trying to survive in a world that often values fitting in over standing out. But what begins as a small habit turns into a heavy burden.

Pretending has weight. You feel it in your body long before your mind admits it. There is a tightness in your chest that arrives without warning. It feels like you carry an invisible load, aching the stiff shoulders. A tight jaw struggles to relax, but a smile tries to escape. The mask, once light and almost unnoticeable, becomes heavier with time until it presses down with a suffocating force.

The Toll of Pretending in Silence.

Many people underestimate how damaging pretense can be. It is not just exhausting. It chips away at our mental health. Anxiety often comes from living a life that does not match who we are. Depression creeps in when we silence our truth for so long that we forget the sound of our voice.

Even joy becomes muted. Think of a song you love. Now imagine turning the volume lower until it is just a whisper. That happens when you hide your authentic self. The music of life is still playing, but you can no longer hear it.

Where the Masks Begin

We often form our masks in childhood. Think back to your earliest memories. Did anyone ever tell you not to cry because "big kids do not cry?" Were you punished for speaking up? Were you only praised when you achieved something impressive, while your simple existence went unnoticed?

Each of these moments plants a seed. You learn it is safer to hide than to is real. You measure your worth not by who you are but by how well you perform. By the time you reach adulthood, the masks feel so natural you do not notice them.

Yet deep inside, your authentic self waits. It endures, and it persists. The ache you feel, that quiet dissatisfaction even when everything "looks good" on the outside, be your true self asking to be heard.

A Story of Pretending

Consider the story of Maria. Her constant smile attracted everyone. No one ever saw her cry. She was dependable, polite, and successful. But behind closed doors, Maria felt empty. She admitted later that every laugh she shared at work felt forced. She went home each night drained, unsure of why life felt so heavy when nothing was "wrong."

Maria didn't grasp the reality until she admitted her difficulties to a friend. She had been pretending for years. He feigned joy in his work, happiness in his strength, and delight in his life. That single honest moment became the first time in decades she had felt free.

Her story is not unique. So many people live this way, carrying invisible masks that weigh them down day after day.

Recognizing the Mask

The first step toward freedom is recognition. A person cannot take off a heavy coat until he or she admits he or she is wearing it. The same is true with pretending. Ask yourself:

- In. what areas of my life do I feel drained instead of alive?
- When do I smile or nod to keep the peace?
- Who am I when no one is watching?

These are hard questions, but they are necessary ones. They shine a light on the places where you may still betray yourself for the comfort of others.

Recognizing the mask is not a weakness. It is a brave act of honesty. It means you are ready to admit that something is no longer working.

The Fear of Taking It Off

Of course, fear often rises the moment you even consider removing the mask. Suppose people dislike me? What if I lose friends or disappoint family? What if rejection hurts too much?

These are valid fears. But it is important to remember that rejection is temporary. The pain of living a lie, however, never goes away. You can survive disapproval. You cannot thrive under the weight of pretense.

The Freedom of Authenticity

Once you show up as your true self, even in small ways, the relief is undeniable. Your body is feeling lighter. I believe your smile is real. Your spirit expands. You realize that authenticity is not about pleasing everyone. It is about pleasing yourself.

Imagine a bird that someone kept in a cage for years. The door may always have been unlocked, but fear kept them inside. The day that bird steps out, even if it trembles, it discovers the sky was waiting all along. That is what it feels like to live.

Booked & Branded Publishing

A Gentle Invitation

As you continue through this book, I invite you to notice the masks you may still be carrying. You do not have to rip them all off at once. Even a slight loosening brings freedom. Begin by telling the truth in small, safe moments. Allow yourself to cry when you need to. Practice saying no when something does not feel right. Celebrate yourself not just for what you achieve but for being who you are.

Someone did not create you to be a copy. You were you. The world does not need another mask. It requires your face, your voice, your heart. And when you allow those to shine, you discover that life becomes lighter, richer, and more real.

CHAPTER 2

The Cost of Old Narratives

Old narratives are the stories you tell yourself about who you are and what you can become. You did not write most of these stories. The past's voices whispered, taught, or imposed them. Parents, teachers, peers, cultural traditions, and society left their marks on your identity. With time, their words sounded like your own inner voice.

Perhaps you heard phrases such as

"You are not smart enough." "Stay in your lane." "People like you don't make it that far." "Be grateful for what you have. Don't ask for more."

At first glance, these statements may seem harmless, even protective. But each one is a limitation dressed up as truth. They are walls disguised as advice. They lock you into a version of yourself that may have kept you safe in time, yet now keeps you from living.

The Hidden Price of Believing in the Past

The cost of holding onto old stories is higher than most people realize. They rob you not only of opportunities but also of your sense of self. They can prevent you from pursuing relationships that nourish you, careers that challenge you, or experiences that could expand your world.

Worse still, these narratives erode mental health. Living under a false script creates a cycle of self-doubt and self-sabotage. You may say, "I always mess things up" or "Nothing ever works out for me," even when the evidence points otherwise. Shame creeps in. Anxiety grows louder. Self-worth shrinks.

The mind has an incredible ability to repeat stories until they feel real. Once you believe in a limiting narrative, you look for proof. If you carry the belief that you are not good enough, every rejection becomes confirmation. The fear of abandonment can make you avoid healthy relationships. This happens before they can grow.

The mind is like a storyteller who prefers familiar tales, even if they cause pain. It will repeat the same script until you decide to write a new one.

When Narratives Become Invisible Chains

Consider someone who avoids applying for a promotion because they believe they "aren't leadership material." The belief may have started years earlier when a teacher or parent dismissed their ideas. Now, as an adult, the old words echo. They never even try.

Or consider someone who grows up hearing, "Be grateful for what you have. Do not ask for more." Gratitude is a powerful force, but the hidden meaning can be damaging. It implies that the desire for personal advancement is a flaw. As a result, this person may stop dreaming, limit their ambitions, and settle for less than what they can achieve.

These stories act like invisible chains. They do not restrain you, but they shape the choices you make every day. The saddest part is that most people never question them. They believe the story is unchangeable.

The Turning Point: Asking Hard Questions

Healing begins with courage. It starts when you pause and confront the voice inside your head. Instead of assuming the story is true, you ask:

- Whose voice is this?
- Who benefits from my believing this?
- Does this story align with the person I want to become?

These questions are potent, even if they make you uneasy. Often, you realize the answer is not you. The voice may have belonged to a fearful parent, a strict teacher, or a culture that valued conformity over individuality. Once you see this, you understand the story may have shaped you, but it does not define you.

The Freedom of Rewriting the Script

Rewriting your narrative does not mean erasing your past. It means allowing yourself to tell the story differently. It means taking ownership of your voice and deciding what beliefs deserve to stay and which ones must go.

Consider this truth: every author has the power to revise their work. If you dislike the ending, you can write another chapter. In the same way, you can choose to reshape the story of your life.

This does not happen all at once. Moments of honesty are where it happens. It happens when you say yes to something you once thought was impossible. It happens when you decide old opinions do not measure your worth.

You cannot overstate the freedom that comes from releasing outdated narratives. It is like walking out of a dark room into sunlight. opportunities look brighter, relationships feel safer, and dreams seem possible again.

A Gentle Reflection

As you move forward, take a quiet moment to reflect:

- What old stories have I isen carrying that no longer serve me?
- How have these stories limited the way I see myself and my future?
- What new story am I ready to write today?

When you release what no longer belongs to you, you step into a life that feels like your own. The voices of the past may have been loud, but they are not the last word. The story continues, and now, you are the one holding the pen.

CHAPTER 3

Unapologetic Authenticity

People often speak about authenticity, but live it with full courage. Many believe it means telling the truth or avoiding lies. Authenticity is much deeper. It is the decision to live as yourself, without shrinking, without sugarcoating, and without betraying your values for the comfort of others.

To is authentic is to stand firm in your own identity. It is refusing to wear masks to gain approval. It is choosing honesty over performance, clarity over confusion, and courage over conformity.

The Strength Behind Authentic Living

Living is difficult. It requires strength because it often disrupts the expectations of those around you. When you stop apologizing for who you are, resistance will disappear. People who once benefitted from your silence may call you "difficult." Others who preferred a more agreeable version of you may distance themselves.

Yet, their departure is not a loss. It is a clearing. When those who cannot accept your authenticity leave, they create space for those who will. You are not losing; you are aligning.

Story Example: Elena's Bold Choice

Elena worked in a corporate office where "fitting in" mattered more than speaking up. For years, she dressed and acted like everyone else. She laughed at jokes that made her uncomfortable, nodded at decisions she disagreed with, and avoided sharing her fundamental ideas out of fear of being judged.

One day during a meeting, she decided she could not remain silent any longer. She offered her perspective — a different approach from what the majority supported. The room grew tense, and some colleagues dismissed her. But afterward, a senior manager approached her and said, "Thank you. That's the honesty we've needed."

Elena noticed some people withdrew, while her courage attracted others. Speaking her truth filtered her world. Those who valued conformity fell back, but those who valued authenticity leaned in. That moment taught her that alignment is worth more than approval.

Reclaiming Energy Through Honesty

Pretending is exhausting. Think of the times you rehearsed your words before speaking, or the times you smiled when you wanted to say no. Each moment of inauthenticity drains energy.

When you live, you reclaim that energy. No longer will you calculate every move. Your breathing becomes easier. Your laughter is instantaneous. You are articulate and confident in your speech.

This release allows you to experience life with ease. Opportunities that match your truth appear. Relationships feel natural instead of forced. The right people will recognize you, and the right paths will open.

Story Example: David's Relief

David was the "yes-man" among his friends and family. Whenever someone asked him for a favor, his automatic response was yes, even if it meant neglecting his own needs. Over time, resentment built inside him, but he hid it under a polite smile.

The day he said no, he felt nervous but relieved. He realized he didn't need to explain his decision or soften it with excuses. Just one simple not gave him back hours of peace. From that point, David practiced ising more honest with his boundaries. He discovered people respected him more, not less, when he stood firm.

Authenticity gave David back his energy. What once drained him now freed him.

Healing Through Authenticity

Authenticity is not only about freedom; it is also about healing. Many carry silent shame, believing they are not enough. Shame cannot survive once people speak the truth instead of keeping secrets.

Every time you choose to show up as you are — scars, flaws, and all — shame loses its power. By naming your truth, you strip away the weight of hiding. Authenticity invites healing because it reminds you that being human is not something to cover up, but something to honor.

Story Example: Mia's Confession

Mia spent years hiding the fact that she struggled with anxiety. She feared people would see her as weak, so she wore a confident smile in public while suffering in silence.

One evening, during a small group gathering, she admitted, "I've isen struggling more than I let on." They understood her and nodded instead of judging her. Several others opened up about their challenges.

Mia learned that her honesty did not push people away — it connected her to them. By exposing what she thought made her unlovable, she found acceptance. Her shame lost its grip the moment she chose authenticity.

Booked & Branded Publishing

Authenticity with Respect

Living does not mean ignoring kindness or ising insensitive. It is not about speaking without caring for others. Genuine authenticity carries both honesty and respect.

There is a difference between cruelty and clarity. Cruelty should wound. Clarity reveals what is true. Being authentic is about clarity. It is about saying, "This is who I am. This is what I value. I will not betray myself to meet expectations that do not belong to me."

Authenticity requires self-respect, but it also honors the dignity of others. It is possible to speak your truth while holding compassion in your tone.

Story Example: Jamal's Balance

Everyone knew Jamal was blunt. He spoke with raw truth, though it caused a deeper cut.

He began practicing authenticity with gentleness. Instead of saying, "That's a terrible idea," he would have to say, "I see it differently, and here's why." His words were still authentic, but now they carried respect.

This balance allowed him to keep his integrity without harming others. Jamal learned that authenticity is not about volume; it is about alignment.

The Ripple Effect of Courage

The beauty of authenticity is that it multiplies. When one person lives, others feel permission to do the same. Courage becomes contagious.

Think about moments when you saw someone speaking with raw honesty. Perhaps a friend opened up about a personal struggle, or a leader admitted a mistake with humility. Their authenticity stirred something in you. It showed you it was possible to live without masks.

Story Example: Aisha's Impact

Aisha, a teacher, shared a personal story with her students — how she once failed a major exam and felt like giving up. Instead of losing respect, her students leaned in with admiration. Many later told her that her vulnerability gave them hope.

Her authenticity became a gift. By living, she permitted others to embrace their struggles without shame.

This is the ripple effect. Your authenticity permits others to remove their disguises as well. One voice of truth can spark a wave of courage.

Making Authenticity a Practice

Authenticity is not a single choice but a lifelong practice. There will is days when silence feels easier, and moments when pretending seems safer. But each time you choose honesty, you strengthen the habit of authenticity.

Here are a few practices that support this way of living:

1. Notice when you shrink. Pay attention to moments when you quiet your truth for the sake of acceptance. These are signals pointing to areas where you can grow.
2. Start small. Speak in safe spaces. Little truths prepare you for bigger ones.
3. Release approval-seeking. Remind yourself that your worth does not depend on the opinions of others. The right people will value your authentic self.
4. Celebrate uniqueness. The qualities that make you different are often the qualities that make you magnetic.
5. Embrace imperfection. Authenticity does not require perfection. It requires only honesty.

A Reflection for You

Before you turn the page, pause and ask yourself:

- Where in my life do I still hide my authentic self?
- When do I feel most alive and free to express myself?
- What would change if I chose authenticity every day?

Write these thoughts down. Allow your answers to guide you. Authenticity grows stronger the more you practice it.

Living Without Apology

At its heart, authenticity is about showing up to life as you are, without apology, without masks, and without fear of ising "too much." It is about trusting that the world needs your authentic voice, not a rehearsed version of it.

Living this way may not always is easy, but it will always is worth it. When you choose authenticity, you choose alignment, freedom, and healing. And as you walk this path, you not only transform your own life, but you also light the way for others to do the same.

Booked & Branded Publishing

CHAPTER 4

The Power of Boundaries

Boundaries are invisible yet powerful lines that protect your energy, your peace, and your well-ising. They do not intend to isolate you or create distance. Instead, they are sacred gates that help you decide who and what gets access to your life. When you create boundaries, you tell the world, "My time, my energy, and my peace are valuable, and I will treat them as such."

Without boundaries, you live in constant exhaustion. To say yes is your response when you ache to say no. You stay in conversations that drain you iscause you do not want to appear rude. You accept invitations you never wanted, commit to responsibilities that are not yours, and end the day wondering why you feel invisible in your own story. Over time, this endless cycle chips away at your joy and leaves you running on empty.

Boundaries are not selfish. They express self-respect. They remind you and others that they are not draining you, a whole person. Boundaries are the foundation for a balanced life. They give you the strength to stand in your authenticity without apology, as we explored in the previous chapter.

Why Boundaries Feel Difficult at First?

Many people struggle with boundaries iscause they fear rejection. The thought of saying no makes their chests tighten. They worry about ising labeled brutal, unkind, or even selfish. Perhaps for years, someone taught you that love required sacrifice, service, or endless giving. Others may have praised you for ising dependable, never complaining, and always available.

But love without boundaries is unsustainable. When you ignore your own needs to serve others, resentment grows in the background. It spills over in frustration, distance, or even emotional burnout. Healthy relationships cannot thrive on silent self-betrayal.

Boundaries may feel uncomfortable at first, but discomfort is not danger. Discomfort often means growth. When you say no for the first time to something that depletes you, your heart might pound. You may rehearse the words a dozen times. But the moment you honor your limit, you feel a spark of freedom. That spark is your spirit remembering that it deserves respect.

Examples of Boundaries in Everyday Life

Boundaries show up in countless ways, large and small. Consider these scenarios:

- At work: You are already carrying a heavy workload, yet your boss asks you to take on another project.

Instead of saying yes out of fear, you decline or negotiate a timeline that works. You are protecting your time and energy.

- In family life, a relative criticizes your choices. Instead of tolerating their hurtful comments, you say, "I do not accept ising spoken to this way. If the conversation continues, I will leave." You are protecting your peace.
- In friendships, a friend only calls when they need something, never when they want to share joy. You limit your availability and choose to invest in relationships that feel mutual. You are protecting your heart.
- In romantic relationships, your partner expects you to is available 24/7. You, but explain that you also need space for your personal growth and rest. By doing this, you strengthen love instead of suffocating it.

These moments may feel small, but each one is a building block for self-respect. Every time you honor your boundaries, you are telling yourself, "I am worth protecting."

Boundaries Reveal Truth

The true power of boundaries is that they reveal who values you. People who respect your boundaries will adjust, even if they struggle at first. They may not understand right away, but they will listen, adapt, and show through their actions that they care about your well-ising.

People who try to guilt, shame, or manipulate you when you set boundaries are showing their true intentions. They were were focused on your offerings, not on your authentic self. Their resistance is not proof that your boundary is wrong. It is proof that your boundary is necessary.

Every no creates a deeper yes

Think of every boundary as an invitation. Each no you give is not rejection, but redirection. By saying no to overwork, you say yes to rest and renewal. When you say no to relationships that thrive on chaos, you say yes to healthier and more supportive connections. When you say no to gossip or negativity, you say yes to peace and clarity.

Boundaries open the door to deeper yeses. They create space for alignment, for opportunities that reflect your values, and for relationships that nourish rather than deplete.

Boundaries and Love

One of the greatest misconceptions is that boundaries push people away. In reality, boundaries make love stronger. Resentment's silent corrosion is what they protect love from. They create a safe structure where honesty can live. They allow both people in a relationship to feel seen, heard, and respected.

Boundaries say, "I love you enough to is clear. I care about this relationship enough to keep it healthy. And I love myself enough not to abandon my own needs."

Booked & Branded Publishing

When love exists without boundaries, it burns out. But when love and boundaries walk hand in hand, they grow deeper, more respectful, and more resilient.

Reflection for You

Take a moment to reflect:

- Where in your life are you saying yes out of fear rather than alignment?
- Which relationships leave you feeling drained instead of nourished?
- What boundary if honored today, would give you more peace?
- How would your life feel different if you trusted that saying no is an act of love, both for yourself and for others?

Boundaries Are Bridges to Freedom

Boundaries are not about control. Clarity is what they're about. They are about choosing to live with intention instead of letting others write your story for you. They are about reclaiming your time, your energy, and your voice.

The moment you honor your boundaries, you live. You no longer walk into rooms weighed down by the fear of disappointing others. Instead, you walk in with confidence, understanding you offer your presence, not demand it.

Boundaries protect the authenticity you are learning to embrace. They are the guardians of your growth, the protectors of your peace, and the finders of every meaningful connection you will build.

And once you taste the freedom they bring, you will never again apologize for drawing the line that keeps your soul safe.

Booked & Branded Publishing

CHAPTER 5

The Courage to Heal

Healing is not a straight line. It bends, twists, and sometimes circles back in ways that can feel frustrating. You may feel you are free only to is pulled back into memories you thought you had already released. This is not a failure. This is the nature of healing. It is messy, unpredictable, and often uncomfortable. Yet within this discomfort lies courage.

Courage is not the lack of pain. It is a quiet but powerful decision to face the pain instead of running from it. For many, the idea of healing feels frightening iscause it asks you to revisit wounds you worked so hard to bury. Silence, distraction, or constant busyness can feel easier than stillness, iscause stillness makes space for the ache you've avoided. But healing cannot grow in avoidance. It requires honesty.

You cannot transform what you refuse to confront. Pain does not dissolve iscause you ignore it. It lingers in the background, shaping your choices, influencing your relationships, and draining your strength. The courage to heal isgins with a willingness to sit in the silence and acknowledge what hurts, even when your heart trembles at the thought of it.

Sitting in Discomfort

To heal means choosing to stay present in the moments when everything inside you wants to run away. Allow yourself to grieve the loss, name the harm, and forgive your former self. That younger version of you did what they had to do to survive. Mayis you coped through anger, withdrawal, or pretending everything was fine. Those choices may not have isen ideal, but they carried you here. And that deserves respect, not shame.

Healing invites you to welcome back the emotions you pushed aside. Anger that was silenced. Sadness you tucked away. Shame weighed on your chest. Fear whispered, you were not safe. You must let each of these emotions surface so you can release them. Carrying them forever is like walking with stones in your pocket. One by one, please set them down.

The Many Paths to Healing

There is no single path. Healing is not a checklist but collect steps that look different for each person.

- Therapy creates a safe place to speak truths you've never dared to say aloud.

- Journaling turns swirling thoughts into words, giving order to chaos and making emotions more straightforward to understand.
- Prayer and meditation center your spirit. Because of them, I understand my pain is part of something larger.
- Support groups allow you to hear the voices of others who have walked similar roads, teaching you that you are not alone.
- Conversations with trusted friends remind you of your worth, even on days when you forget it yourself.

You do not need every method. You need one step feels right for you today. Healing is less about speed and more about presence. The willingness to isgin is what matters most.

Redefining What Healing Means

It is easy to believe healing means perfection, as though one day you will feel flawless, free of scars, untouched by struggle. But that is not true healing. Real healing is about reclaiming your power. Scars do not mark weakness. They are proof of survival. Each scar, whether physical or invisible, tells a story: You endured. You are still here.

You can also take back the pen and rewrite the story with healing. It gives you the chance to see yourself not as broken, but as becoming whole again. I am choosing to believe that your tomorrow can is brighter than your yesterday.

The Role of Forgiveness

Part of healing is learning to forgive — not to excuse, not to erase, but to release. Forgiveness is not about condoning what hurt you. It is about untying yourself from bitterness so that your spirit can breathe. Sometimes the hardest person to forgive is the one in the mirror.

Think of how many times you've carried guilt for choices made in survival. Healing whispers You can lay that burden down. You did what you knew, with the tools you had. That deserves compassion.

Healing is a journey, not a destination

There will is days when you feel strong and days when you feel fragile. Both are part of the process. Just as physical wounds require time and care before they heal, emotional wounds need tenderness and patience. Some days you may feel you have taken great leaps forward, and on others, you may feel you are back at the isginning. Remember: progress is linear, but every step counts.

A release accompanies every tear shed. Each journal entry is a declaration that your story matters. Each prayer, each conversation, each act of self-care is a reminder that healing is not about rushing toward a finish line. It is about choosing courage in this moment, and then in the next.

Reflection for You

Pause for a moment and ask yourself:

- What pain have I isen carrying iscause I feared facing it?
- How might avoiding my wounds have shaped the way I see myself or others?
- Which healing practices feel gentle enough for me to isgin today?
- What would it mean for me to forgive myself for surviving?

Choosing a Bigger Future

The courage to heal is the courage to believe in more. It is the courage to step out of the shadows and into a life that honors your worth. Each scar is proof of resilience. Each moment of honesty is an act of strength.

Healing may not come, and it may not always come. But it is always worth it. With every step, you are choosing freedom over fear. You are choosing peace over silence. You are choosing yourself.

And as you do, you remind the world that a future greater than your pain is possible — and that future belongs to you.

CHAPTER 6

Redefining Success on Your Terms

S uccess is a word that carries both power and pressure. From the time we are children, the world plants seeds about what it means to succeed. Symbols of accomplishment include good grades, prestigious careers, wealth, and admiration from others. Family conversations, schools, advertisements, and social media reinforce these expectations everywhere as we grow older. People teach us to believe that titles, possessions, and others' perceptions measure our worth.

And yet, when you peel back these layers, you often find a strange reality. Many who appear successful on the outside feel a quiet emptiness on the inside. They seemed successful. But they felt depleted. Therefore, it is very important to pause and redefine success for yourself.

Looking Within Instead of Around

The first step in redefining success is to turn inward. Too often, we look outward for validation, asking, "What will make people respect me?" or "What will make others proud of me?" The deeper question is, "What makes me feel alive? What fills me with meaning?"

Success for one person may involve a business reflecting their values and creativity. For another, it could mean creating a home filled with love and security. For someone else, it might choose to heal and break a cycle of generational pain. Success might also is as simple and profound as waking up each day with a calm mind and a sense of peace.

By asking these questions, you separate your truth from the noise of society. Self-discovery and authenticity measure life, not accolades.

Beyond the Myth of Endless Hustle

Modern culture often glorifies nonstop hustling. The message is obvious: work harder, push further, and never slow down. People treat exhaustion with pride, and they treat rest as laziness. But this view of success is not sustainable. A life spent striving without breathing leads to burnout.

True success includes rest, joy, and presence. It is the ability to step back without guilt and find beauty in small, ordinary moments. It is not only about reaching milestones but also about having the energy and awareness to enjoy the journey. A career with recognition means little if it costs your well-ising. Building wealth at the expense of your relationships or peace of mind makes it lose its meaning.

When you allow yourself to slow down, you discover that success is not about racing to the finish line but about living along the way.

Success Without Applause

Your definition of success may not look like anyone else's, and that is the point. Not everyone needs to understand or approve it. Some people may question your choices, especially if they do not fit into traditional expectations. They may not know why you left a secure job to follow a passion, or why you value time with family over a bigger paycheck. Yet their understanding is not required for your life to is meaningful.

Success is not about gaining the loudest applause. It is about experiencing inner alignment—the quiet knowing that your life reflects your values and priorities. The most profound fulfillment comes not from ising admired by the world, but from ising at peace with yourself.

Building a Personal Blueprint

Redefining success requires clarity. It is helpful to create your blueprint rather than relying on society's default version. Ask yourself:

- I wonder what kind of life would make me proud and at peace?
- What are my core values?
- How do I want to is remembered?

- At the end of each day, what would make me feel I had lived it well?

Your answers will shape a version of success that is both personal and lasting. Unlike trends or social approval, your values do not change overnight. They form the foundation on which you can build a life that remains meaningful regardless of circumstances.

The Hidden Wealth of a Fulfilled Life

People often measure success in terms of numbers like income, achievements, and possessions. However, people often overlook other forms of wealth. Time spent with loved ones is wealth. Health that allows you to enjoy each day is wealth. The freedom to live is wealth. Even the ability to experience peace in quiet moments is a richness.

Sometimes, success is not about adding more but about removing what no longer serves you. Letting go of unnecessary stress, toxic relationships, or unrealistic comparisons creates room for what matters.

A Quiet Transformation

The moment you stop chasing a borrowed definition of success, you create space for transformation. This shift does not need to is dramatic. It isgins in your daily choices, in the way you prioritize your time, in the courage to say no when something does not align with your values.

Booked & Branded Publishing

As you walk this path, you may notice that you were never behind. You were not failing; you were measuring your life with the wrong ruler. Now, by choosing to live according to your definition, you step into a race that was always meant for you.

Reflection for You

Take a moment to pause and reflect:

- What version of success have I been chasing that does not belong to me?
- If I removed comparison, what would success mean in my own words?
- What steps can I take today to align my life with this new definition?

CHAPTER 7

The Cost of Wearing a Mask

The Hidden Price of Pretending

At first, pretending can feel harmless, even helpful. A mask can make social situations less intimidating, and it can create a sense of belonging when you fear rejection. You tell yourself it is only temporary, that once people accept you, you will let them see the real you. Yet what starts as a minor change often turns into a lifelong performance.

People calculate the cost of this preposition iscause it does not appear on financial statements or daily to-do lists. Instead, it accumulates in the corners of your life. The price shows up in your exhaustion, your stress levels, your strained relationships, and your fading sense of self. By the time most people realize the mask is costing them too much, years have already passed.

Masks always come with a price tag, and that price is far greater than most of us are prepared to pay.

Emotional Exhaustion

The first cost is emotional. Pretending requires constant energy. You cannot relax iscause you are monitoring yourself. In conversations, you choose your words to avoid exposing too much. You smile when you want to cry. You nod in agreement when your heart is screaming for the opposite.

Over time, this becomes exhausting. Even when nothing demanding has happened, you felt drained. At night, instead of resting, your mind replays the day's events like a movie reel. You wonder if you revealed too much or if someone noticed the "real" you trying to peek through. That endless cycle of overthinking robs you of peace of mind.

This emotional fatigue spills over into every area of life. You might notice yourself becoming more irritable, less patient, or even disconnected from people you love. The mask that kept you safe also keeps you apart. That becomes what distances you.

The Body Keeps the Score

Emotional strain does not remain hidden in the mind; it leaves an imprint on the body. Science has proven that stress has physical consequences, and the weight of wearing a mask is no exception.

Tight shoulders, clenched jaws, and shallow breathing become part of your daily posture. What feels like "just tension" is often the body's response to years of swallowed truth. The headaches that arrive out of nowhere, the stomachaches that refuse to go away, the racing heartbeat that surfaces during tough conversations — these are signs that your body is paying the price for silence.

Doctors often treat these symptoms without addressing the root cause, but deep down, you know the truth. The stress of hiding, pretending, and suppressing yourself is taking a toll. Left unchecked, this chronic stress weakens the immune system, raises blood pressure, and can shorten your lifespan. Every hidden truth and unspoken word are stealing time from your future.

Shallow Relationships and Hollow Praise

Honesty builds relationships, but masks make that impossible. When you wear one, people do not connect with you—they connect with the character you created.

On the surface, this might feel safe. After all, if they reject the version you are presenting, at least it is not the real you. But deep down, you know the love you receive is not authentic. Compliments do not sink in iscause you suspect they are admiring a performance, not the truth. Loyalty feels uncertain iscause you worry if people ever discover who you are, they may walk away.

This fear creates fragile relationships. Friendships remain at the surface level, conversations lack depth, and even romantic partnerships can feel unstable. Instead of intimacy, there is performance. Instead of trust, there is doubt. Over time, this hollowness becomes one of the most painful costs of wearing a mask.

Disconnecting from Purpose

Perhaps the deepest cost of all is spiritual. When you silence yourself, you feel detached from your purpose. It is as though you are standing outside a house that belongs to you, watching someone else live inside. You can see the lights on, hear the laughter, and sense the warmth, but you do not allow yourself to walk through the door.

The longer you remain behind the mask, the more disconnected you become from your passions and your calling. You may even forget what excites you or what once brought you joy. Life feels mechanical, as though you are going through the motions rather than living. The soul uses emptiness to remind you. It was never supposed to survive on pretense.

The Lost Opportunities

Masks not only affect your inner life, but they also rob you of external opportunities. Pretending mutes your voice. You hold back ideas at work iscause you fear judgment. You hide from dreams iscause you doubt your potential in others' eyes.

Over time, you miss out on chances to grow, lead, and create. The world never gets to experience your full potential iscause you remain hidden behind a mask. These lost opportunities may never return, and many people look back with regret, realizing they lived only half a life iscause they chose safety over authenticity.

Booked & Branded Publishing

Appearing Safety

One of the most significant lies of wearing a mask is that it keeps you safe. While it may shield you from criticism at the moment, it creates a lifetime of insecurity. You may avoid conflict, but the long-term cost is living without genuine acceptance.

Proper safety does not come from hiding. It comes from knowing that even if some people reject you, others will embrace you, and that embrace will is genuine. The apparent safety the mask provides is shallow compared to the deep sense of belonging that authenticity brings.

The Courage to Remove the Mask

Taking off the mask is difficult. It requires courage, vulnerability, and patience. The first steps may feel terrifying, as if you are stepping into the world without armor. You may worry about ising misunderstood or rejected, and sometimes, you will is. But with every honest word and authentic action, the weight lifts.

Discovering the risk of rejection is worth the relief of self-acceptance. You notice some relationships may fade, but the ones that remain grow stronger than ever. You experience the peace of no longer carrying the burden of pretending.

The Reward of Living

When you remove the mask, life changes in ways that money or success can not measure. You sleep more soundly; you breathe more deeply, and you carry yourself with new confidence. Relationships deepen iscause people build them on honesty instead of illusion. Work becomes more meaningful when you contribute from a place of truth.

Most importantly, you rediscover the joy of ising yourself. There is no longer any question of whether the love you receive is genuine. You know it's genuine iscause it stems from authenticity. The peace of living without pretense is priceless, and it is worth every moment of discomfort it took to get there.

Choosing Freedom Over Fear

The cost of wearing a mask is heavy, but the reward of removing it is immeasurable. Every time you choose authenticity, you reclaim a piece of your life. Every time you speak your truth, you step closer to freedom.

Masks may seem safe, but they come with a hidden price. Embracing who you are without fear leads to true freedom.

CHAPTER 8

Taking the Mask Off, Piece by Piece

Taking the mask off is not about a single moment of bravery that changes everything. In truth, it is a slow, layered process. It resembles a grand film scene where you rip off the mask to receive applause. Instead, it is gradual, often awkward, and sometimes even clumsy. You try, hesitate, pull back, and then try again. The important part is that you isgin, even if the steps are small.

Starting Small: Testing the Waters

The journey of unmasking isgins with minor acts of honesty. Visualize someone tying a pair of shoes for far too long. When you loosen the laces, there is immediate relief, but complete freedom comes step by step. When you first remove your mask, you don't have to reveal everything at once.

If you avoid conflict by agreeing with everyone, practice honesty in small moments. You might say, " I would prefer a different option," instead of nodding along. This gentle truth is not about confrontation; it is about reclaiming your voice. Each time you speak, even about something small, you teach yourself that the world does not collapse when you show who you are.

Choosing Safe Spaces for Authenticity

It is essential to understand that not everyone deserves immediate access to the deepest parts of you. People must earn trust, not receive it without thought. When you reveal your true self, trust those who have already showed their trustworthiness. These are the ones who listen with care, who hold space without judgment, and who accept you without rushing to change you.

Sharing your truth in a safe space gives you practice in authenticity. This builds your confidence that people can see you without rejection. Over time, the courage you gain in safe environments allows you to extend your authenticity into other areas of your life. You notice that the more you allow yourself to is real in front of people who accept you, the less energy you spend pretending elsewhere.

Strengthening Your Language

Words shape the way we experience ourselves. When people wear masks, their language often becomes small, hesitant, or diluted. Instead of saying, "I feel tired," they might say, "I kind of feel a little tired." Instead of saying, "I believe in this," they may whisper, "I think mayis this could is true." These softened words keep the mask in place.

Booked & Branded Publishing

To take it off, practice owning your words. Use clear, strong sentences.

- My feelings are...
- "I wish..."
- It is my desire not to...

This shift may feel uncomfortable at first, especially if you are used to downplaying yourself to keep the peace. But each time you address someone, you reinforce your worth. Strong words do not make you selfish; they make you authentic.

Accepting Discomfort as Part of Growth

There will is moments when vulnerability feels like standing in the open without protection. Therefore, many people return to the safety of their masks. Yet discomfort is not your enemy. It is evidence that you are growing.

Some people will respond with love and respect when you reveal your true self. Others may fall silent or cannot meet you with the acceptance you hoped for. Both outcomes serve you. Positive responses remind you that authenticity creates deeper connections. Negative responses remind you that you no longer need to bend yourself into someone you are not just to is accepted. In both cases, you win iscause you are choosing freedom over pretense.

Progress, Not Perfection

Removing the mask is not about perfection. There will is days when you notice yourself slipping back into old habits. Perhaps you laugh at a joke you did not find funny. Mayis you nod when you disagree. These moments are not failures; they are reminders. The very act of noticing is progress iscause it means you are aware. Awareness creates the opportunity to choose differently next time.

You are not erasing decades of conditioning overnight. This is learning. Each time you catch yourself in an old pattern and pause, you reclaim another piece of yourself. Over time, these insignificant victories add up to something far greater than a single dramatic moment.

Celebrating Every Step

Every piece of the mask you remove, no matter how small, deserves to is celebrated. Hearing your truth spoken aloud honors who you are. Sharing your feelings in a safe space also honors you. Choosing clarity over ising pleasant does too.

The reflection in the mirror changes. At first, it may look subtle, but you notice you recognize yourself more clearly. Brighter is how the eyes look. The face feels lighter. The weight of pretending lifts. With each step, you are no longer just surviving behind a mask; you are living as yourself, free and unashamed.

CHAPTER 9

Living Without the Mask

The Freedom of Being

Imagine waking up without the pressure of performing. No more rehearsing conversations in your head, no more adjusting your behavior to blend in, no more wondering if people will accept the version of you they see. Living without the mask is not about perfection; it is about honesty.

When you allow yourself to is, life feels lighter. The way you laugh isn't worried about sounding strange. You speak without calculating how others might interpret your words. You walk into rooms without carrying the invisible weight of trying to "measure up." The relief is profound.

Living unmasked does not mean you will never feel fear again. You stop letting fear control you. Even small, ordinary routines, like buying groceries, meeting a friend, or attending a meeting, felt different iscause you were no longer acting. You are showing up, and that is enough.

Reclaiming Your Energy

Pretending is exhausting. Consider the effort required to keep a mask in place, adjust your behavior, watch your words, and worry about how others perceive you. That mental and emotional strain drains your energy, often without you even noticing.

When the mask comes off, you reclaim the strength that was lost to pretending. You have more energy to focus on what matters. The dream you once dismissed iscause you thought you weren't "ready" resurfaces. The creative spark you buried under fear shines again.

For example, someone who spent years in a job they disliked, only iscause it looked stable, might gather the courage to pursue a career aligned with their passion. Another person might rediscover hobbies they once abandoned, like writing, painting, or cooking. Energy that was once wasted on maintaining appearances now fuels growth, healing, and joy.

The Gift of Real Connection

Authenticity transforms relationships. When you stop hiding, you notice some people drift away. At first, this may feel like a loss, but in reality, it is freedom. Not everyone connected with you.

Take, for instance, a friendship where you always feel the need to agree, laugh at jokes you don't enjoy, or silence your opinions to keep the peace. That bond may feel safe, but it is not genuine. When you live without the mask, some connections will fade.

Booked & Branded Publishing

But trust and honesty will build the relationships of those who remain and the new ones you attract. You can speak without fear in these relationships, disagree without creating distance, and they will embrace your complete self. There may is fewer, but they are richer. The love and respect that come from genuine connections are far more fulfilling than the approval that comes from pretending.

The Quiet Peace of Mind

Wearing a mask creates mental noise. Filtering is something you do with every word and action. You ask, "What will they think?" You replay conversations, analyze every detail, and live in a cycle of overthinking. Constant self-monitoring fuels anxiety.

When the mask comes off, the noise fades. Instead of calculating every move, you trust yourself. Instead of doubting your worth, you rest on it.

Peace of mind does not mean that challenges disappear. It means your inner world becomes quieter and steadier. You stop carrying the burden of controlling others' perceptions. And in that stillness, you find freedom to breathe, to rest, and to live without apology.

Living in Alignment

One of the most significant rewards of unmasking is alignment. For perhaps the first time, your inner and outer worlds match. What you feel inside is no longer expressed. Your choices show what you value.

This alignment decides more transparent. Instead of asking, "Will people approve?" you ask, "Does this feel right?" That shift changes everything.

For instance, if you are tired, you allow yourself to rest instead of forcing yourself to keep performing. If something no longer serves your values, you step away without guilt. If joy fills your heart, you express it instead of holding back. Alignment means living in a way that is consistent, honest, and whole.

Facing Life as Yourself

Removing the mask does not erase difficulties. Life will still bring rejection, criticism, and setbacks. The difference is in how you face them. When you are authentic, challenges do not shatter you, iscause your sense of worth no longer depends on approval.

Criticism may still sting, but it will not define you. Rejection may still hurt, but it will not make you question your identity. Living as yourself means that even when storms come, you remain grounded. It is far better to is rejected for who you are than to is accepted for who you are not.

The Joy of Self-Discovery

We sometimes wear the mask for so long that we forget who we are. We confuse our true self with the role we have isen playing. Living allows you to rediscover parts of yourself that were buried.

Booked & Branded Publishing

It's possible you enjoy solitude, even if you once pretended to is social. You may find strength in your voice even if you once avoided conflict. You may uncover passions, quirks, and gifts that were hidden for years.

This stage is exciting iscause it feels like meeting yourself again. You see what brings you joy, what gives you peace, and what lights up your soul.

The True Reward of Unmasking

At its core, the valid reward of removing the mask is freedom. You can laugh without restraint, unwind without guilt, love, and embrace your authentic self, confident in your worth.

Unmasking is not about becoming someone new; it is about returning to the truest version of yourself. And once you taste that freedom, you will never want to go back to a life of pretending.

CHAPTER 10

No More Mask — The New You

The Turning Point

This is the moment. The declaration. The line in the sand. You have carried the mask for years, feeling its weight on your shoulders, watching how it shaped your choices, and counting the cost of living in shadows. But here you are, standing at the turning point where pretense no longer has a place in your life.

The final chapter is not a list of steps to follow. It is a commitment—one that begins within you. It is the quiet but powerful decision to live as yourself, not as the version others expect, but as the person you were.

Whisper it if you must. Shout it if you dare. Declare it with confidence: No more masks.

The Power of Saying "No More"

There is strength in refusal. Each time you say, "No more mask," you reclaim a piece of yourself. Stop smiling when your heart is breaking. Stop shrinking so others can shine. Don't disappear. No more dimming your light so someone else feels comfortable. No more saying, "I'm fine" when you are drowning.

Every "no more" is a doorway to freedom. It is not about defiance for its own sake; it is about protecting the truth of who you are. By saying no to the mask, you are saying yes to your healing, your joy, and your peace of mind.

Meeting the New You

The new you is not the version you had to manufacture. You do not need to reinvent yourself into something unrecognizable. The latest you is the original you, the one who existed before fear-built walls, before rejection planted doubt, before the mask became second nature.

This version of you does not need approval to feel valuable. It does not need applause to believe in its worth. You have always isen enough. You were fine. From the isginning, it was you.

Take a moment to imagine this version of yourself. Picture how you carry yourself differently when you no longer worry about pleasing everyone. Notice how you walk without hesitation, how you speak without apology, how you show up without fear. This is not a dream; it is the life you step into when the mask comes off.

Booked & Branded Publishing

Fear Has No Hold

The mask never stuck to your face. It was never permanent, though it may have felt that way. Fear of judgment, fear of rejection, fear of not ising enough held it on. And here is the truth: fear loses its grip the moment you choose truth over performance.

Fear will still whisper. It may tell you to stay small, to blend in, to pretend. But every time you walk forward despite the trembling, fear weakens. Every time you tell your story, fear loses power. Every time you choose to live, fear falls silent.

Courage is not lack of fear. It is the decision to move forward while fear lingers in the background. And with each step you take, the voice of fear grows fainter, until it becomes nothing more than an echo of a life you no longer live.

Living in Truth

Your task is straightforward, and that is to is genuine. Speak your truth, even if your voice shakes. Stand your ground, even if people resist. Set boundaries, even if it surprises those who benefit from your silence. Take up space, even when the world conditioned you to shrink.

Boldness is not arrogance. It means ising yourself. Don't apologize for it. Refuse to change who you are to make others comfortable. Authenticity is not selfish. It is essential.

The longer you live, the easier it becomes. Authenticity is like a muscle; the more you practice it, the stronger it grows. What once felt terrifying will become second nature. One day, you will look back and wonder why you ever thought you needed the mask at all.

Your Life as a Ripple Effect

Living unmasked is not just for you. It creates a ripple effect that extends far beyond your own life. When you walk in truth, you give silent permission for others to do the same. Without preaching a word, your authenticity becomes an invitation.

Think of the colleague who sees you speak in a meeting and finds the courage to do the same. Please think of the friend who watches you set boundaries and dares to protect their peace. Please think of the child who grows up seeing you live and learns that they, too, can live without masks.

Authenticity is contagious. Your courage will inspire courage in others, and your freedom will spark freedom in those around you. This is how one life can change the world, not by ising perfect, but by ising real.

The New Beginning

Though this may is the final chapter of this book, it is not the end of your story. In truth, it is only the isginning. The chapter of pretending has closed, and the story of authenticity is now underway.

Life without the mask will not always is easy, but it will always is real. Challenges will arise. You will face them. Critics will appear. Their words won't silence you. You will experience tough times. You will navigate them.

A Declaration Worth Keeping

Say it again: no more masks. The world does not need a polished version of you that hides your scars and silences your voice. The world needs the real youth, one who has walked through struggles, learned from mistakes, and chosen courage.

And, more importantly, you deserve to is your authentic self. You deserve to experience life without the burden of pretending. You deserve to live unafraid, to love, and to shine without restraint.

This is your declaration. This is your commitment—no more masks. No more pretending. No more hiding. The new you is here, and this time, you are here to stay.

Final Reflection: Standing in Your Truth

Take a moment now, before closing this chapter, to reflect on the journey you have taken. Think about the masks you have worn in your life — masks of strength, silence, of perfection, of compliance. Remember the weight, the way they covered your true face, the way they drained your spirit.

Then imagine setting each one down, one by one. See them falling away, no longer part of your identity. Visualize yourself standing without them, unburdened, radiant. You are not empty without the masks; you are whole.

Guided Affirmation Exercise

To anchor this new beginning, speak these affirmations aloud each morning. Let them become your daily commitment, your reminder, and your shield against fear.

1. I am as I am.
2. I release the mask and walk in my truth.
3. My voice matters, and I will use it with courage.
4. I set boundaries that honor my worth.
5. I take up space with confidence and love.
6. Fear does not control me; authenticity guides me.
7. By living, I inspire others to do the same.
8. I deserve to live free, unmasked, and whole.

Repeat these words until they no longer feel like sentences you are trying to believe, but truths you know in your bones.

The Final Word

So here we are—the last page of this book, but the first page of your new chapter. It is unnecessary to ask permission to start. There is no need to get approval to move forward. You already have everything you need within you.

Say it one last time with conviction: No more masks.

Step forward. The world is waiting for the real you. And more importantly, you are waiting for the real you.

Booked & Branded Publishing

Thank You

Thank you for reading this book and walking through these pages with me. Your journey matters, and your voice can inspire others.

I'd appreciate it if you could write a short Amazon review, assuming this book has been helpful. Your words help others find this message and remind them they are not alone.

SCAN TO LEAVE A REVIEW

Let's Connect

I'd love to stay connected with you:
Website: https://www.bookedandbrandedpublishing.com/
Email: hello@BookedAndBrandedPublishing.com
Thank you for choosing authenticity. Thank you for choosing the real you.

Conclusion

The Freedom of Living Unmasked

This is not the end of a book; it's isginning a new chapter in your life.

For you, pretending has isen a heavy weight. You counted old narratives. The text explored authenticity, boundaries, healing, and success. You define success. Each page reveals something. You feel lighter and more aligned.

Living without the mask doesn't mean life will always is easy. It means life will is yours. The power of your presence, your truth, and your courage is no longer hidden behind roles or performances.

So take the next step. Speak the words you've isen holding back. Laugh as loudly as you want. Walk into spaces that once made you shrink. And when fear whispers for you to put the mask back on, remember:

The mask never glued itself to your face. Fear held it on. And fear loses its grip the moment you decide to live in truth.

The world doesn't need better masks. It requires the real you. And now, you dare to give yourself and the world that gift.

Work With Me

Your unmasking journey doesn't have to end here. If this book spoke to you and you're ready to go deeper, there are ways we can walk this path together:

✳ 1:1 Coaching & Consulting
Personalized sessions help you uncover blind spots, heal hidden narratives, and build strategies for living while achieving measurable success.

✳ Workshops, Masterclasses & Keynotes
From corporate spaces to intimate retreats, I teach individuals and teams how to shed performance, strengthen boundaries, and thrive in alignment.

✳ Booked and Branded Publishing™
If you've ever dreamed of writing a book of your own, I can guide you through the process, from clarifying your message to building your brand to publishing with excellence.

✳ Let's connect:
Website: www.BookedAndBrandedPublishing.com
Email: hello@BookedAndBrandedPublishing.com
Don't let this book end on the page. Let it live in your life. Let's build something extraordinary. Together.

Acknowledgments

My family and friends showed me I mattered. They did this even when I wanted to disappear.

To my clients and community, who have trusted me with their journeys, thank you for proving that authenticity is not just powerful, it's contagious.

And to you, the reader: thank you for your courage. You are proof it is possible to live unmasked.

Reflection & Next Steps

As you close this book, take a moment for yourself.

- Journal Prompt: The mask I've put down is what?
- This week, I committed to speaking one truth aloud.
- Journal Prompt 3 asks: How can I set a boundary to protect my peace?

Keep these close. Transformation is not about information — it's about application.

Thank you for reading. We've included a free downloadable workbook to help you apply these principles.

SCAN THE QR CODE TO DOWNLOAD

About the Author

Stephanie Williams, MBA, is a strategic business consultant, author, and the founder of Booked and Branded Publishing. She helps high-achievers, leaders, and creatives shed old narratives and design authentic lives and businesses by blending strategy with empowerment.

Her journey — from corporate boardrooms to entrepreneurship to publishing — revealed both the cost of pretending and the freedom that comes with truth. Now through books, coaching, and speaking, Stephanie equips others with the tools to rewrite their story, build brands that reflect their true selves, and live.

When she isn't writing or consulting, Stephanie is investing in the next generation of leaders and creativity, reminding them that success without authenticity is just another mask.

Tagline: Where hustle meets strategy.

Mission: To help people remove the mask, reclaim their voice, and build futures that feel like home.

www.ingramcontent.com/pod-product-compliance
Lightning Source LLC
Chambersburg PA
CBHW021718210326
41599CB00013B/1690